SMOKE & MIRRORS

SMOKE & MIRRORS

MAURICIO MEJIA
with SHAREEN RIVERA

Paperback ISBN: 9798615882784

Editor: Shareen Rivera
Published by Rising Above Publishing Services

Contents

Acknowledgment

first want to thank GOD for all the blessings and opportunities given to me. I also want to thank my mother, father, sister and my family for being in my life and showing me, no matter what, we're family.

I do want to thank my industry colleagues, my friends, the party people in Miami, Las Vegas, Los Angeles where is it all started for me and the Bay Area (San Jose, San Francisco, Oakland) and to all that have stayed by my side, business mentors, and coaches. Nothing I've accomplished would be possible without the support from you. I truly thank you and love you all.

Last but not least, I dedicate this book and the many more to come to my 3 boys. Andrew, Mekhi and Kayson, dad loves you!

Foreword

When it comes to the epitome of overcoming obstacles, creating positive outcomes, navigating complications, being true to his loved ones, and celebrating life with generosity...well, that is the essence of Mauricio Mejia.

Every day is an adventure. It might start with some Latin music, laughter, and genuine concern for any of his enterprises and any member associated. Having shadowed him for several days, I can attest to that with complete validation. From morning to evening, there is style, focus, and conscious consideration regarding how to DECIDE – COMMIT – EXECUTE – which is his mantra and process for developing and delivering a dynasty.

His charisma is catching and creates smiles. His intensity has the propensity to throw a whale into a tailspin. His gentle nature and ability to see and accept others and show love, in my opinion, differentiates him from many leaders and phenomenons.

Smoke and Mirrors conveys what is real or what is a façade. What you get with Mauricio is authenticity, integrity, honesty, excellence, and grit that is unsurpassed. He is willing to learn, grow and live life full out. In his presence, as a reader or participant in his programs or venues, the energy will resonate within you. You will elevate to more of who you are.

With deep gratitude,

Kristin Andress

Author – Entrepreneur – Speaker…..and one of Mauricio's friends and greatest fans. He will impact your life…perhaps even change it.

Message From
the Author

This is the first time I've ever told my story. My intention of doing so is with hopes that it resonates and inspires someone with the same hunger that I felt growing up, someone with a parching thirst for more in life. I hope you read this book and believe that if I can do it, you can too. It's not easy existing in this world. The struggles are real, but if you can hold on to your drive, anything is possible.

Introduction

How the fuck did this happen to me?! How the fuck did I get here?! My head was spinning, and all I could repeat to myself over and over were these two questions. I stood in my marble shower naked, broke, alone—very alone, and felt the grasp of fear that I was running from so desperately. I never knew what it was like to lose. For the first time in my adult life, I had lost—lost it all in the blink of an eye. I made my first million and became a self-made millionaire by 25 years old. Here I was now 32 and had lost it all.

The more I tried to hang on, the more everything spiraled out of control. All the events that led me up to this point were flashing through my mind. Even though I had never felt self-pity or allowed myself to play the victim in any manner, I couldn't help but feel sorry. I let my body slide against the clear glass shower door until I was curled up on the marble floor with my head on my knees letting the warm water wash it all away. Wash away my pity. Wash away all the fears that I let accumulate inside of me until it was like a huge ball in my throat that I couldn't push down, constantly reminding me of what was going to happen, of this very moment that I was dreading. I let the water rain over me, cleansing my soul of all the sins I committed that I believed came back to haunt me.

The tears and the water from my shower were all I had at that moment. I let myself feel sorry. I let myself feel pity. I let myself feel scared and dread of the unknown ahead. I let myself feel it all in that one moment because I knew the second I got out of that shower I had to face the world. I had to return my keys to my beautiful loft in the heart of Japantown in San Jose, California, and I had to start over. I allowed myself that one moment though to break down because I knew it was time to rebuild. Rebuild from the ground up.

Even though I didn't know how I was going to do it, somewhere inside of me beneath the fear and dread, I believed I would because I've done it before. I started from literally nothing, and I knew I could do it again. It was time for me, Mauricio Mejia, to dig deep down into my soul and pull out that young, ambitious, curious, and inspired teenager who was hungry and believed he could. It was time to reintroduce that man who was in me to myself again.

1

The
Launch

"Chele! Chele," my mother yelled as she swung my bedroom door open. "Chele, get up!" It was a school day morning in Monrovia, California. At 15 years old, I wasn't about to get up any earlier than I had to. As I tossed in bed irritated, my mother yelled again, "Chele, get up, there's a Lamborghini outside. A red one. Get up!" I knew then she had to be messing with me. There's no way a red Lamborghini, just like the one on the poster hanging above my bed, would be outside of my house, especially in my neighborhood. "Sure, Mom," I said as I turned my back to her to sleep another five minutes. "I'm serious, there's a Lamborghini outside." I figured I had to get up anyway, so I sluggishly got out of bed and followed her unenthusiastically to the front room to entertain whatever game she was playing. As I peered through our front room window there was, in fact, a red Lamborghini in front of our house.

"Holy shit!" I yelled as I ran back to my room searching for my polaroid camera. I had to take a picture of myself in front of it and show my friends at school. I knew there was no other way they'd believe me. I rushed to get myself ready and ran outside with my camera.

In the naive and inexperienced mind of a 15-year-old, I didn't think it was more than a coincidence that the same exact red Lamborghini that I laid in my bed staring at night after night showed up in front of my house in a Monrovia neighborhood. I didn't know anything about manifestation or the Law of Attraction, but I am convinced that is exactly what had happened twenty-seven years ago; which coincidentally, happened to be Valentine's

Day. I had no idea as I ran outside to take this picture that my life was about to change forever.

I went to school beyond thrilled, showing off my pictures and telling all my friends the grandiose story of the Lamborghini in front of my house. As I walked home that afternoon, I anticipated it would be gone, but as I got closer to my house, I saw it was still there in the exact same place. There were two guys looking under the hood as if they had no worries or care of what neighborhood they were in with this luxury vehicle. The curiosity thrilled me, and I approached them wanting to know more.

"Is this your car?" I asked with as much confidence as I could muster without revealing the uncontrollable excitement I felt inside. "Yes, it is," one of the guys said as he was looking in the trunk located in front of the car. They were both Latino guys in their twenties who exuded confidence, finesse, and excitement. They were Martin and Albert who I later found out were known as part of the "Teddy Boys."

Albert looked like a big-time drug dealer and surprisingly lived across the street from my house in the gated apartment complex. And Martin, well Martin was just a cool guy. He had big green eyes and looked like a Latino model, and because of that, he was welcomed into any nightclub because he attracted the females. When I asked them what they did for a living to be able to afford this type of car, his answer was promoting.

This was a time before social media and the Internet. This was a time and generation where you didn't have immediate access to find out what the latest trends or styles were. You either had it or you didn't. Martin and Albert definitely had it. That OG natural type of cool swag, and oddly enough standing next to them, I did too. Albert was sitting in the front passenger seat wearing a white V-neck shirt with rolled-up sleeves and ripped jeans. The vibe between us three was immediate, and before I knew it 15-20 minutes had passed and I felt completely comfortable with them. They invited me out with them that night and said they'd pick me up at nine.

I walked inside my house in absolute disbelief that this was happening. The profound feeling of the situation being so surreal would be unbelievable to anyone and was almost overwhelming. I had no idea what I was going to wear or even what people wore to clubs. I didn't know what to expect at all. I nervously got ready and changed what seemed a million times before I settled on wearing a white V-neck shirt, blue jeans, and Doc Martin boots— something similar to what I saw Albert wearing.

I sat and tried to watch TV while waiting, but I couldn't concentrate on anything. My house was empty. My mom was working as usual. She was a hairdresser and worked tirelessly around the clock to keep a roof over me and my sister's heads. Consequently, I was alone and came and went as I pleased without having to answer to anyone most of the time. It was that exact freedom that molded my curiosity in life and paved my path for my future.

Martin and Albert arrived right at 9 p.m., and as I walked outside, it didn't even occur to me how three people were going to fit into a Lamborghini that sat only two people. The doors lifted up, and all I could hear was the music blaring. Martin came out of the front seat and ushered me in; no words were said or needed. I sat on the floorboard of the passenger seat, Martin pinned to the right side, and at that exact moment, there was nothing weird about it. We were in a fucking Lamborghini flying through the streets to Los Angeles. We speeded past all the normal, ordinary cars with ordinary people living their ordinary lives. Speed was irrelevant. We were in a fucking Lamborghini. All three of us were on a different vibe, and I felt more alive than ever yelling as we flew over the bumps and sped around the corners.

I thought the ride there would have been the highlight of the entire experience that night until we arrived at the nightclub. All I could see was a line of people down the street, block after block, wrapped around the building. Music was coming from all of the cars driving by. It was The Red Onion, a chain of Mexican restaurants turned nightclubs at night. This one was located in the San Gabriel Valley's East of Los Angeles, City of West Covina, and my first taste of real nightlife took place.

Martin handed me an ID and said it was for protocol purposes and not to worry. I looked down at this ID. It was a Jose from Salinas who looked nothing like me at all. Not even close! Even though he said not to worry I thought, *what the fuck?*

We pulled up to the front of the club, and as the doors lifted up, I could feel the eyes of thousands of people on us. There were two lines: one for 18 and over and another for 21. Both lines wrapped around the building. I got out of the Lamborghini dumbfounded and immediately followed Martin and Albert's lead. As we walked up, the security guard and several other guys greeted them and opened the velvet ropes. No one asked me for my ID. Shit, they barely even looked at me, acting as if they didn't see me or notice how young I looked. It didn't matter if I was carded or not.

Everyone in the line was glaring at us, hating me with their eyes and wondering who the fuck I was to be walking in like I was VIP. I loved it and stood there as if I belonged exactly where the fuck I was—walking in before them without even being carded. The mystical power of making people wonder who you are was absolute magic to me and completely transformed my mindset, level of confidence, and perception of myself.

As we walked in, I could hear Naughty by Nature playing. The bass of the music flowing through my body relaxing my nerves just called me to come in and play. I immediately knew this was where I wanted to be. Whatever Martin and Albert were doing, I wanted to do.

We walked up to our VIP table, which was in the second room of the club that DJ Muggs from Cypress Hill was playing. Bottles of alcohol were waiting for us, and not one person asked who I was. They even poured my drink without question. Girls immediately came to the table, taking me off the couch to dance. I was in absolute heaven for a 15-year-old kid who was just lying on his bed the night before staring at his Lamborghini poster.

By the end of the night, I no longer gave a fuck about being out on the streets getting caught up in shit. I no longer gave a fuck about going to these lame parties kids had from school. After that night, I would never care again about any of this stuff. My mind was made up. The seed had been planted, and from that point on, all I cared about was getting into the nightlife that Martin and Albert were into and getting the connections and being known like they were at the places they were known at. My mind was on getting that money, and that is exactly what I set out to do.

2
Get Hungry

One year after meeting Albert and Martin, my life had spun rapidly out of control. At just 16 years old, I was deep into the nightlife. I had already started becoming a street promoter for a few clubs, and my circle of friends no longer consisted of just normal kids from high school. It had broadly expanded to the streets, drug dealers, club promoters, and women.... lots of women.

I was learning first-hand the LA style of promoting. I wasn't just some punk kid on the streets handing out flyers. With Albert and Martin, I was learning how to exude their level of confidence, and how to execute "in your face" style of promoting— a style that I made my own as my career progressed. I learned in this type of business, it wasn't about who you were, but who others thought you were. We would roll up to places in Albert's Lamborghini or Mercedes, catching as much attention as we could. More eyes on us the better. By the time people got ahold of my flyers, they were so intrigued they felt like they would be missing out if they didn't show up.

While my social life had grown, my home life was falling apart. My mother was notorious for getting into toxic relationships that always ended with our lives being turned upside down and starting over. This time, she had gotten involved with a married man and somehow this relationship had cost her our apartment and, once again, we were about to become homeless. Even though I wasn't fond of our apartment that got infested with cockroaches from time to time, I still, at just 16 years old, needed the emotional and physical security of having a home.

My sister and I had no idea what was going to happen to us. Nothing seemed to deter my mother's ways of handling things. She looked for love in all the wrong places and handled her problems the same way.

The stress and uncertainty at home combined with late nights and partying on the regular started to catch up to me. I was feeling lost and out of touch with myself. I craved structure and discipline, and I knew no one was going to enforce that in my life. So I took it upon myself to seek it on my own. Even at a young age, I knew something bad was going to happen if I didn't find a way to create some type of balance in my life. I enrolled myself in the LA County Sheriffs Cadet Program, a boot camp type of program that required all participants to show up at 6:00 a.m., dressed, and ready to go. I knew this was exactly what I needed, and I did everything I had to do in order to stay enrolled in the program, including cutting my sideburns. For me, that was huge. I was desperate for structure.

While I kept myself occupied with my street promoting, school, social life, and boot camp, I was still dealing with the fact that we were being evicted, and I had no idea where I was going to live in a few weeks. One day my mom told me she had arranged for me to stay with her friend Tim Nugent, a movie editor in Hollywood. He lived in a nice house and I knew him, well, kind of. I didn't know where my sister and mom would be, but I couldn't worry about that. I agreed, and a few days later, I was to pack all my stuff to move. I was used to this kind of lifestyle. Ever since I could remember, I had been moving and left with my mom's "friends" who were more like acquaintances.

I was left with a young teenage girl at eight years old while my mom worked. My mom told me she knew her. At eight years old, I didn't know any better than to do what I was told. When my babysitter told me to touch her and let her touch me, I hesitated but listened. I was eight when I was first exposed to sex. Not knowing if it was right or wrong or who to tell, I just shrugged it off as nothing. I didn't play with trucks and cars like other normal boys. I played with my sister's Barbies...naked Barbies, pretending they were having sex because I had already known what men and women did at that age. Instead of seeing this as a sign that something was wrong with her son, my mom ignorantly laughed and used to make jokes about it when I got older. It was then that my emotional ties to women had been tainted by the immoral decision making on the part of the women who were in my life. It was something I had grown accustomed to dealing with and started expecting from women, but also something I learned from a young age to protect myself from as well.

Moving in with Tim wasn't so bad. I had my own room in a very nice house in a great neighborhood. Tim was a good and hardworking man, plus he didn't really bug me about my whereabouts. I had a routine going on and more structure than I had in the past year. On the weekends I would go with him to Hollywood with him to his office behind the Star Search building. I would sit for hours learning how movies would be edited and learned to appreciate having patience. Long hours, and watching the same things for hours and hours until perfection. It all ended as soon as it began, and once again I was to be uprooted.

One night I was coming home from boot camp. I was tired, sore, and starving. All I could think about was throwing myself in my bed. As I was walking uphill to the house, I could see Tim's son Dan yelling at his dad in the driveway. As I got closer, I could see he was on one. Tim was yelling at him and before I knew it, Dan ran up to his father and knocked him out cold. I heard Tim's head hit the pavement and watched Dan as he ran inside. I was petrified and in complete shock. I yelled out Tim's name and shook him trying to wake him up. I thought he was dead. I had no idea where Dan was but was sure as soon as he saw me, he was going to try to fuck me up since I saw the whole thing. I ran up the stairs to my room. I grabbed a steel baseball bat and shut the door and turned the lights out. I was ready and waiting for him right by my bedroom door. Honestly, I was ready to kill him with this bat. There was no way I was going to let some fucking punk touch me.

Sure enough, I heard his footsteps up the stairs, yelling you fucken spic, you wet back, and a bunch of other crazy shit. As he got closer and the handle turned. He flicked the light on, and his glazed over, wide eyes immediately found me standing there staring straight at him, gripping that bat, ready to attack. He knew I wasn't playing. I knew my eyes said everything. I didn't have to say shit. We both stood there staring at each other for a good minute before he slowly backed up and turned the light off and shut the door.

I stood there until I could hear the sound of his footsteps fade, and when they did, I dropped the bat. My whole body was shaking. I immediately got some of my stuff and ran out of the house. I ran past Tim's body still lying on the pavement. I ran as fast as I could down the street to a phone booth at a 7-11. My mind was racing because I knew I couldn't go back to living at Tim's house. I didn't even know if Tim was alright. I didn't know what was going to happen to me. I knew my mom wasn't able to help me. I remember feeling so alone and desperate.

I don't know how I remembered my cousin Raff's phone number who lived in the San Francisco, but I did. I don't know why he was the first person who popped into my head to call, but he was. As I look back, I know this was the Universe's way of leading me to my destiny.

I made a collect call and was praying he would answer. Sure enough, he did. As soon as the operator connected us, I heard his voice. "Chele, are you ok?" I felt a huge weight being lifted from my shoulders. I frantically explained to him what happened and how I didn't know what I was going to do. He put his brother Eric on the phone, who was a CHP officer. "Chele go to the nearest police station and tell them everything you just told us. It'll be okay. Don't worry. Call us as soon as you can when you're there and we'll figure out how to get you up here." I knew there was a police station not far from the 7-11. I was already exhausted and dreading having to go through all this bullshit, but knew I had to. "Don't worry," Eric repeated in an attempt to reassure me.

That night was the moment my life had changed dramatically. I was to move in with my cousins in the Bay Area for an unknown period of time. I was to leave all that I knew in LA. With so much uncertainty lying ahead though, I still felt hopeful inside. Something inside of me knew it was going to be alright. I was going to find my way just like I always had. A decision was made that my sister would come with me to the Bay Area as well, and my Mom drove both of us up north.

The reality of our broken family hidden behind the fake conversations carried such a sad energy in that car ride, but nothing was more profound than that big elephant in the car: the why we were in this situation to begin with. I knew my mom was too stuck in her way of life and didn't know any better. Naturally, I still had resentment, but she was still my mom and deep down I understood. I understood her better than she may have understood herself, and because of that, the big elephant was tucked away and overlooked for the sake of my mom's sanity.

I looked out the window on Interstate 5 for most of the ride up. No matter what I was thinking about, the one feeling that wouldn't go away was a deep, rotting, wretched feeling of disgust. The kind of disgust that makes your stomach feel like it's turning into knots.

I was so utterly disgusted with how life had been so far. Disgusted with the instability and uncertainty being a routine part of the normalcy in my life. Disgusted with toxic, evil people pretending to be innocent and fronting with their fake ways. Disgusted with not having my own place to live so I could feel safe. Disgusted with living whatever lifestyle life throws my way, even if it meant living with cockroaches in my house. I was just utterly disgusted with the struggle.

I refused to accept that this is what my life was going to be—that this was going to continue to be my normal. As I sat there looking out the window, I was determined to use this disgust to propel me to do something about it out in the Bay. I was determined for the cycle of poverty, ignorance, and victim of life mentality to change with me. I knew the only way I was going to do that was by taking some kind of action with what I knew, and what I knew was promoting. I knew how to be disciplined. I knew I was smart enough to use my wit to figure out how to change my life and that is what ignited the spark of hope inside that I felt beneath the thick layer of disgust. A hope that became a belief, the belief in myself.

As I hugged my mom goodbye, I didn't know I wasn't going to see her for another few years; otherwise, I probably would have made it a more memorable parting. I knew she felt just as helpless as we did, so I kissed her on the cheek goodbye and walked away without any words that would rub in guilt or despair. I saved that energy to focus on starting my new life, my new life in the Bay Area.

3

Fake It till you make it

n the first few months living with my cousins in San Francisco, there were many changes happening so rapidly that my mind couldn't process it. I was in shock trying to adapt to it all. I hadn't fully accepted the fact that this was my permanent home. I wasn't able to accept that I would have to let go of everything I once knew and leave the place where everyone knew me in order to start over somewhere else.

I knew no one and no one knew me. A combination of denial and rebellion motivated me to believe I would attend school Monday through Friday and then find a ride to LA every weekend. This one idea gave me a sense of security. I wanted to believe this was one part of my life I could hold on to, and that was my circle of friends in LA and the excitement of that nightlife's "glitz and glamour" that came with it.

My sister went to live with my aunt and uncle who lived in Richmond. Knowing she was safe off the streets and living in a household with structure gave me peace and acceptance of the fact that we were going to be permanently separated.

My cousins Raff and Eric were well into their 30's and living in a house in San Francisco. My mother signed over full guardianship of me to them so they could enroll me in the high school nearby. My mother giving up guardianship wasn't something that sunk in at first. It was just another transition at the time that had to be done, but as time went on and my mother was nowhere around, I came to fully realize and accept that she was no longer a part of my life.

My cousins enrolled me in Westmoor High School, and after six months of attending school and doing nothing else but what was asked of me, I decided it was time to check out the nightlife in San Francisco. I already had my fake ID that said I was 21 years old. It wasn't one of those fake IDs that all the other kids had. I had this ID since I was 15 years old, and it was from the DMV with my picture on it. I could go and do anything I wanted with that ID. I noticed immediately the distinct difference between the nightlife in San Francisco and the nightlife in Los Angeles, and I knew what San Francisco needed was me. I had that LA, in your face, bold attitude, and nothing about San Francisco nightlife had that. The music was all house. The crowd was mainly White. If there were any Blacks or Latinos they were artsy or educated, nothing wrong with education, it just wasn't my thing. There was no club that offered a mix of music where an intermingled crowd could come together comfortably and enjoy themselves. It was missing the LA edge that brought no color lines.

I immediately approached the general manager at the first club I went to for 18 years and older, City Nights in San Francisco. My level of confidence combined with my gift of gab had this guy convinced I could pull off what San Francisco needed, and it would be a hit. He agreed to let me hold and promote an event on a Sunday night there, SWEET SUNDAYS. Even though I didn't know how I was going to pull it off, once again I just believed in myself enough to know I would. I've always had this strong faith in myself that no matter what happens, I'll make that vision in my head transpire into reality. It is that exact faith that has always been the crutch I lean on whenever obstacles are thrown my way.

I failed miserably with this event, but with that failure were valuable lessons. First, I was able, at 17-years old, to convince the general manager of the club to hold an event he'd never done. That just validated the belief in myself that my gift of gab was a real thing and my age was completely irrelevant. Second, I realized I didn't know how San Francisco's nightlife and crowd worked. I approached it like it was LA, but San Francisco definitely wasn't LA and neither were the people. I learned that everything in the Bay Area functioned differently and had to be approached like so. I knew, though, once I learned how things worked, I'd be unstoppable.

Before the end of my junior school year, I had turned 18 years old because I was held back in the second grade. When I was younger I got jumped at school, and we sued the school for it. I ended up being awarded a settlement that I would get when I was 18, and the money came at the perfect time. I was close to the end of my junior year, and I needed a car. Of course, I wasn't going to buy just any old looking car like the rest of the kids my age. I ended up buying a convertible 1969 VW Karmann Ghia convertible, black with a purple pearl paint job and Porsche alloy rims. It was sick!

One day as I was washing my car on a warm spring day at my friend's house in Richmond, California, and as I was finishing up, I saw this beautiful woman starting to wash her car. Being the over the top confident kid I was, I offered to wash it for her, and she took me up on the offer. As I was washing her car we were talking, and she asked me what I did. I said, "I go to school," in a very matter of fact tone without hesitation, knowing she was much older than me and praying she wouldn't question what school. She didn't. The combination of the kind of car I drove, my maturity, the way I looked, and my level of confidence was enough for her to think I was much older than I was. She assumed I was in college instead of high school. Our connection was magnetic and powerful. We started dating immediately.

She was everything I could ever imagine a real woman to be. She was beautiful, sexy, classy, intelligent, and stylish. She was also 11 years older than me. Her age though is what attracted me more to her because she gave me that sense of security I longed for. Her maturity brought wisdom and stability, both of which I yearned for.

The night I knew I was in love with her was on our first date. We went out to the Sound Factory in San Francisco. The line was wrapped around the building, and as we were walking up, I could see a look of dread on her face. She headed towards the end of the line telling me, "Well I guess we'll have to wait in the line." I pulled her back and told her I don't wait in lines. She gave me a dumbfounded look and confusingly asked, "What do you mean?" I told her to wait right here while I talk to the bouncer. I boldly walked up to the bouncer and started with my gift of gab. I told him I was a promoter for a club called Roxy in Hollywood and asked if they offered club courtesy. I was willing to pay but I didn't want to wait in the line. He said, "Yeah, of course." I walked back and took Patricia's hand. The bouncer lifted the red velvet rope as we approached, and we walked right in. As I shook his hand, I passed him a hundred-dollar bill that was folded in my palm.

That night was just as life-changing as the first time I went to a club in LA with Albert and Martin.

I was only 18-years-old but completely taken by this woman. She loved to dance, and it didn't matter if it was alone or with me. I watched her body sway to the music as if they were one. It was mesmerizing watching her get lost in her own place to the music dancing And even more captivating was the way she looked at me as if I were her Prince Charming she had been waiting for.

I didn't know all that would be required of me when a woman looks at you like that, but I didn't care. I felt like I'd do anything to keep her in my life, to keep that look she gave me that made me feel like a man. We started seeing each other regularly and going out every weekend. We weren't just going to the clubs like a regular couple. No, we were going to the VIP sections of the clubs with the owners, who's who, and performers. Our energy together bolstered each other's confidence and kept everything exciting and new.

Soon after meeting Patricia, my cousins and I had a falling out. I wasn't obeying the rules of their house because I was never home, skipping school, and coming in at all hours of the night. I didn't give a fuck about their rules or any rules. To me, there were no limits or rules that applied to me. I was a hot-headed, angry teenager with a rebel without a cause attitude. They kicked me out. Once again, I found myself uprooted, having to move schools, and regain stability. Of course, my mom was nowhere to be found, and even though my father lived in San Francisco, I hadn't even seen nor heard from him since moving there.

My cousins arranged for me to stay with my other cousin in San Pablo. To top it all off, because I was 18 years old, the school district wanted to send me to a continuation school to graduate. I wasn't having that. I had to do something. I knew there was no way I would graduate without the structure of high school. I wasn't going to allow myself to be another Latino kid from LA with no diploma.

So as I went to get my grades from my teachers at Westmoor High, my English teacher asked me what grade I thought I deserved. I looked at her in the eyes and confidently told her an A. She didn't laugh or hesitate but immediately wrote an A on the paper. My history teacher forgot to write the grade in the box, so I figured since I already got an A, I might as well put a B in there. I thought it was believable enough not to be questioned since the grades for my other classes were average.

I took my report card and personally brought it to the principal at El Cerrito High School. I was ready to do what I had to do to convince this guy to let me into the school. I introduced myself and explained the situation. I apologized for being held back in the second grade but told him as tears filled my eyes, I needed to go to school to graduate. I knew he knew he'd be the biggest fucking prick if he didn't give me a chance, so he agreed and patted me on my back as I left his office. I knew I didn't fit in, and I didn't give a fuck. I had facial hair, dressed older than I was, drove a nice car, was an adult and able to write my own excuses to leave school, and had connections that no one at any school had. I stood out, but I aroused everyone's curiosity so much that they wanted to get to know me.

One night after Patricia and I were intimate, I just knew I had to come clean and be honest. I told her that I was going to tell her many times before, but after a night out, I had that liquid courage and decided to just say it. "I want you to know something," I said softly. She looked at me with big eyes, scared of what I was going to confess. "I'm going to be a senior this year"., "I know," she said. I said, "A senior in high school." She pulled back from me just staring at me in shock. "I thought you meant college when you told me you were in school." I confessed I knew she thought that, but I also knew she wouldn't give me a chance if she knew the truth. "Does it really matter though?" imploring her with my eyes to see past it.

She did see past it. Our age difference didn't matter, nothing did, because at that point we both were already in love. For the next 13 years, Patricia was always the woman I couldn't deny. Our relationship was tumultuous, on and off all the time, but she was always the woman I'd go back to every time to feel safe. The woman that felt like home. I never could give her the security and loyalty that a mature man could, but Lord knows I tried for an 18-year old kid.

I graduated with my class from El Cerrito High School with just Patricia and my cousin in the audience. Even though my mother, father or sister weren't there, I didn't give a fuck. I had made it and was looking forward to starting the Upward Bound program at San Jose State that summer that allowed new freshmen to live on campus in dorms for a few weeks. I felt like I could start finally living my life in the real world.

I didn't really think about what would become of Patricia and me after I went away to college. I just knew as I saw her out in the audience, I appreciated her presence in my life. She was out there supporting me during my graduation when my parents weren't, and that meant more than words could say.

I learned that day that the Universe always brings to you the right people at the exact time that you need them. But, out of all the lessons I learned from my relationship with her, I realized you can't fake it till you make it in every aspect of life. There are some things where you just have to be honest and real with yourself and others and accept everything for what it is, especially to the few people who come along your journey and really love you because it's rare. I was just too young at the time to understand it.

4

Fail to
Success

San Jose, to me, was like a smaller version of LA: the people, the vibe, the parties, the fast pace feel of the city life. It didn't take me long to decide I wanted to attend San Jose State. I knew San Jose was where I needed to be. A little while after starting the Upward Bound program, my cousin told me I was not welcome to come back to his house. His wife and I had a falling out after I basically told her to go fly a kite after she tried to place rules on me when I went back there for the weekends (since the program was Monday through Friday). I understood why my cousin didn't welcome me back. He had to stand up for his wife. And I should have been more respectful. It just seemed that life was going in every direction for me and I was lost. Once again, for the fourth time as a young adult, I had no home to go back to. I hung up the payphone thinking, *fuck them all.* I didn't want to rely on or need anyone ever again from that point forward. Everyone's opinions and rules were just bullshit to me and were nothing more than a nuisance.

I went back into my dorm room and sat at the edge of the twin bed folding my clothes, and oddly enough, I wasn't really stressing about any of it. I brushed all of my feelings away and focused on systematically folding everything in a neat pile so I could stack them in such a way where all of my possessions fit into my laundry basket. I'd lay my socks and underwear down first, then my shirts and pants, and afterward I'd lay my towel over all of it so it looked neat.

I had lost my car, was living in a dorm temporarily, adjusting to using the common bathrooms, had no income except the few hundred dollars a month from promoting, and that I could fit all of my possessions into my laundry basket. I still knew I was where I needed to be. I was meeting new people, getting the real college life experience, and was relieved of the burden of having rules placed on me by family members. I relished in my freedom even though it was hidden beneath the restraints of not knowing what would come next.

Shortly after my cousin told me I couldn't come back to his house, I met the founding fathers of a Berkeley fraternity called, Gamma Zeta Alpha, who kept talking about a guy from LA who worked at the radio station, Power 106. It just so happened in passing that we met. By luck, chance, destiny, or whatever you want to call it, my meeting David Garcia happened at the perfect time. We hit it off immediately, and soon after, he told me I could crash on his couch during the weekends I had to be out of the dorm.

Every Friday I'd go through the routine of fitting all of my possessions into my laundry basket and take a bus and then BART to Berkeley carrying my laundry basket with me. The same routine on Monday mornings. I did this the whole summer.

The solitary moments on the BART and bus were the only real moments I ever had to myself. I'd sit by the window lost in my thoughts. I knew where I was at, and what my reality was, but I also knew I was meant for more. The excitement of college life and every new person I met was bringing me one step closer to the top. I already knew bigger things were in store for me; I had already claimed it in my head. It was the thrill of getting there and not knowing how it was going to happen that kept me on my toes.

That summer, David and I got close and realized we could make shit happen together. I also met another guy that summer named Mondo Millian who did promotions for the owner of Hamburger

Mary's in San Jose. We set up a party called Groovy Sundays, and I finally had some money coming in. We created flyers that no one else was doing to promote our parties. Everyone at San Jose State got one and word started getting around. I was creating a name for myself.

The friendships I had created had come to fill that void of not having a family. During the holiday vacations of my freshman and sophomore year, I'd travel back to the East Bay and stay with David because our vibe and energy was like no other. It was then that I truly learned that blood doesn't always equal family.

The Latino fraternity at San Jose State was trying to recruit me for my freshman year. Even though I knew that is where I would fit in the most, where I should be while attending San Jose State, I also knew that there was too much political tension that the brothers were involved in. Proposition 187 had just passed in California. It was a statewide initiative that placed restrictions on illegal immigrants from using our healthcare and public education. Even though I didn't agree with this initiative, I also didn't want to get caught up with the Latino fraternity in placing my energy in it either. My focus was on trying to figure out how to put money in my pocket. In my mind, I had bigger problems to deal with, and the Latino fraternity was just too serious for me.

I started my freshman year living off of financial aid and in the dorms. My first roommate in the dorms turned out to be from LA, Peter Mellado and I became friends quickly and he jumped on board with me in doing promotions. Soon after, to the Latino fraternity's disappointment and the opposite of what all of the other Latinos were doing, I joined an all-White fraternity called Theta Chi. My focus was on expanding the target of people to bring to parties and clubs I would be promoting. The more variety of people I could get connected with meant the more money in my pocket eventually. This fraternity was completely different than the Latino fraternity. Not only was it in a real fraternity house, but the culture was just different. It was all about having fun, parties, drinking, girls, and of course, education, but the energy vibed with mine.

By the end of my freshman year, I had brought in so many Latinos to the fraternity that the population was mixed and it was no longer an all White fraternity. I had also started a party with David and Billy Vidal called Funhouse Thursdays at the Tropicana in San Jose. It was a party like no other during that time. It was the first Thursday party for under 21, and it became so popular that they moved it to Friday nights too. Billy Vidal was like a big brother to David and by default he became my big brother. I learned a lot from him. His back ground was music and radio. He was a former radio jock on 106.1 KMEL in San Francisco and DJ for all the hot parties in San Francisco. Coincidentally, our first encounter was not a good one, and we still laugh about it today. But I'll save that one for later.

The nightlife in San Jose didn't have a memorable tone or culture at that time. There was no social media to hype a party up. We brought that tone with the Funhouse, and I made sure that every flyer we made had that "in your face" LA attitude about it. We stood on the street corners handing out our flyers, put them on cars, gave them out at bars, or wherever we were at. It didn't matter.

By the end of my sophomore year, I had problems in the fraternity with one of the brothers. I was cocky, stubborn, and had an attitude problem, to say the least, and the brothers voted not to let me cross over. I was to leave the summer before my junior year. Once again, for the fifth time, I had no home. I immediately started making calls, and Mondo told me he knew a guy, Jorge, the owner of the restaurant Chacho's, who was renting out a room.

I met Jorge, and we immediately hit it off. He told me the room wasn't much, it was called a dungeon for a reason. It wasn't much, but the rent was affordable, the location was great, and our energy vibed. It was like meeting an old friend when we . met. Soon after moving in with Jorge, my Funhouse parties were extended throughout the whole weekend. I was being reached out to to promote parties at other clubs. I was so focused on my career, my grades at school were dropping, and I was put on academic probation. It became a cycle, and school started feeling like a burden weighing me down and in the way of me getting ahead. I decided at the end of my junior year with one more year to finish school, to quit. Even though it was a huge decision that almost felt like a loss, I knew I was wasting my time because I was no longer fully invested in college.

During that time, I had built a really good relationship with the assistant for Harry Evans, the owner of Tropicana and many other nightclubs in the South Bay. I would go into the office to pick up my cash every week and found out she was leaving. I thought it would be a great opportunity for me. I would get to know the ins-and-outs of the nightlife and really learn the business and promotion end of it. I wanted to immerse my entire life into what I loved, and Harry Evans became a father-like figure to me. At his assistant's recommendation, he hired me as his assistant. He took me under his wing and started teaching me about the business side of nightlife.

While walking in Harry's shadow, my dreams were becoming bigger and bigger. I saw what he was doing and what he had, and I wanted that.

Jorge soon moved out of the house and let me take over the whole house. I turned Jorge's house into a true bachelor party house. I rented out the rooms to a few buddies, and my house was "the house" of East San Jose.

My crew and I would scatter ourselves throughout downtown all week long after 5:00 p.m., handing out our flyers and promoting my parties. My spot was always on Santa Clara Street and Market, right in the heart of Silicon Valley. As I was handing out the flyers, I'd always see the old San Jose Savings and Loans building. It was an old historic building with terra-cotta masonry tile and high-rise black oval-shaped windows with matching tall black glass doors. Not only was it in a prime location in downtown on the main street, but it had the look. I knew that was my building. I would hand out those flyers and tell everyone that this was going to be where my club would be one day. I spoke it out to the Universe, believed it with a powerful hunger, and soon the Universe would yield to my dream.

5

The Handshake

t was a hot August morning in 2003, and I had decided that today was the day I was going to make it happen. I stood looking at myself in the mirror wearing my navy blue suit, handmade Spanish dress shoes, and striped blue and white tie. I felt as confident as ever. I had more money in the bank than I'd ever had before, driving a fully loaded SUV and I was determined to set out and find a way to make my dream happen.

My days at Tropicana had ended, and my time was spent promoting Club Miami and a few other clubs. I was also contractually managing a strip joint in San Jose called Zuatica, which was not as glamorous as I had initially imagined it would be. I was no longer feeling challenged, stimulated, or fulfilled, and I knew it was time to set the bar higher.

I looked at myself and said, "Why not me? Why not now? I can do this. I will do this." I repeated this mantra over and over as I set out to the building in downtown San Jose. I kept my focus on my mantra and refused to entertain any doubtful or fearful thoughts trying to sway me otherwise.

As I went to open the big glass door, an old man opened it before me, and immediately said, "Welcome." I was a little taken back, expecting to see a building with people and employees. I walked inside and looked around and immediately knew this was it. This was the building my first club had to be at. This was exactly how I imagined it would look

Inside, the layout reflected the early century architecture with its wide-open floor plan of about 5,000 square feet, a high ceiling, and a wrap-around stairway that led to a smaller upper level. It was perfect.

The old man's name was Walt Hoefler and he was running his small business called Coast Funding. He bought the building out of bankruptcy and had turned it into his personal office. It was just him in this huge, beautiful building. He was ecstatic to have someone come inside, and even more excited to be with somebody who was curious about the building and willing to listen to his stories.

I sat in his office listening to him explain how the building was a historic landmark and the history of it and downtown San Jose. He just went on and on, telling story after story, more excited than the last as if he hadn't spoken to anybody in years.

I was still taken aback that this whole time this building had just been a personal office space. While we were conversing, I started telling him I was interested in leasing the building and turning it into San Jose's first Ultra Lounge. I explained why it would be a success. San Jose needed a nightclub that would change the current nightlife culture because the city was still stuck in the grunge culture of the late '90s, and now that we're out of the dot com bust, people needed somewhere nice and high-end they could dress up and go to at night. Currently, there was nowhere that was meeting that need.

He listened with wide eyes, nodding his head with excitement at all of the ideas I had for the club and building. The deal was done on a handshake—a simple handshake. I looked at him in his eyes and confidently told him with conviction, "I won't let you down. This is going to be the greatest Ultra Lounge Silicon Valley has ever seen." He put his other hand on top of mine and told me he believed me and instructed me to draft up a letter of intent.

I walked out of that building feeling surreal. I knew this was more than a coincidence. I knew this was pure manifestation at work and that everything that had ever happened to me had led me to this one moment that I was in. It was now up to me to do what I must do to make my dream happen with this one opportunity. I immediately started making phone calls to get everything going. I knew the first big hurdle that I had to tackle was getting the licensing in place. Harry's consultant, Sandra, referred me to her daughter, Aimeé Escobar, and told me she would be able to help me with this project. To this day Aimeé is a close confidant in my life and was right by my side throughout the whole project.

Five months later I got my real estate license and was doing real estate during the day and promoting Club Miami or running the strip club at night. I was constantly on the go, hustling every single day and putting everything I had towards the project.

Soon after, I had a falling out with Jorge's father about the rent for the house, and Aimeé and I became roommates in a two-bedroom townhouse located in Japantown. I had to downsize my life tremendously to make this happen. Harry pitched the project at $300,000. I had anticipated a half million. After all the estimates were done, the entire project was going to cost 1.2 million. I was short by $900,000, and I had no idea where I was going to come up with that kind of money until the contractor fronted me the cash on just my word. As soon as I thought that I had gotten over the biggest hurdle, which was money, the city had denied my final permits for occupancy.

The strip club was not just mentally draining but was an emotional mess. There were ten of the most beautiful women of San Jose, but they couldn't seem to get through one night without any kind of drama. I was constantly being bombarded with problems that I'd never dealt with before. Yet, I had to portray that I knew what I was doing, but really, I had no idea. I was getting phone calls throughout the day while I was out doing real estate dealing with boyfriends, ex-boyfriends, client issues, catty problems amongst the women, and personal and emotional problems. I didn't know what role I played. Some days they wanted me to be a shoulder to cry on, other days the bodyguard, and other days a therapist.

I decided to assign one of the women as the "house mom" to help me out and alleviate some of the shit I was dealing with. I couldn't wait to get out of that place, and when it was time to hand the keys back right before my club opened, I did it anxiously and yet one hundred percent sure I would never get involved in strip clubs ever again.

6

The Vault Ultra Lounge

On Thursday, July 29, 2004, we had the grand opening of the Vault. All my friends, family and colleagues stood around clapping in praise. My two business partners who were part-owners with me on the project stood by my side—Doug AKA Dougie Fresh, who was the manager of the bar, and Regina who we referred to as the "Queen Bee of Los Gatos" who brought in all of the good looking people. Of course, Harry was behind the scenes. Everything felt just right.

Advertisement for the club was done by flyers, and of course, I oversaw the design and layout. This was a time before social media, before any popular Internet platform to advertise anything on existed.

Our first weekend would determine if my theory of the people of San Jose and the Silicon Valley wanting an upscale nightclub to go to was accurate or not.

That Thursday we had our first opening night for friends and family only, and it was sold out. Friday and Saturday night was for the general public. It was sold out. Every weekend after that for the next eight months—SOLD OUT.

The Vault instantly became the place to go to at night. Everyone who was anyone walked through my doors. The first 12 employees of Google came in for an outing, politicians, U2, Madonna, Black Eyed Peas, Jamie Foxx and other comedians after their show at the Improv, plus performers after their show at the SAP Center, athletes, and any celebrity who was in the Bay Area visiting.

I had to deny entry to Barron Davis one night of the Golden State Warriors, because he showed up in white sneakers. Everyone around me was asking if I knew who he was, and I adamantly told them so everyone to hear, "I don't give a fuck who he is, there are no white sneakers allowed." I wanted the bouncers and everyone to understand that there were certain standards set for my club because we were trying to instill a new culture in the down-town San Jose nightlife. I knew if I let him in with white sneakers, regardless of who he was, then I was going to have let the next guy come in with sneakers too. I didn't want any special passes of the culture being given out regardless of title, status, or fame.

Every weekend there was a line of high-end cars parked in front: Lamborghinis, Ferraris, and my red Spider Ferrari included. The cash was rolling in with the Vault at night and my real estate ventures during the day. Bruce Wayne during the day and Batman during the night. My life was starting to become one long, never-ending party. The Vault opened doors to connections of other club owners, and I was starting to get introduced to the lifestyle of owning a club.

My week consisted of working real estate Wednesday, Thursday Friday, and Saturday during the day; at the nightclub Thursday, Friday, and Saturday nights, and then getting on a plane with my crew and flying to Las Vegas until Tuesday to join all of the other club owners in deflating from the long week and discussing ideas that work and don't work with our clubs. That was my life for the next few years, and I had no time to care for anything or anyone.

A few years later, people I considered dear to me had left. My circle had changed dramatically. That's what happens when you start raising the bar for yourself. It was through this transition in my life I learned that not everyone is meant to stay permanently. Everyone has a reason and a season.

One Sunday I sat on the plane with my friends all around me on our way to Vegas, our usual routine, and I looked out the window reflecting on how crazy my life had become within one year. A slight smirk glazed over my face thinking about how I could have never imagined how I now had access to anything and everything. I finally achieved my dream, but it still wasn't enough. I felt like I was on a constant adrenaline rush—excited every single day when I got up out of bed and ready for the next adventure. That's what every day seemed like, one big adventure. Yet, a small part of me still yearned for more. A small part of me was still not satisfied or content, and no matter how busy I was, that feeling remained consistent when I gave myself time to reflect.

I pushed it back into my mind like I do any uncomfortable thought and refused to entertain it. Little did I know those little uncomfortable thoughts I had throughout my fast pace lifestyle were about to accumulate and reveal themselves sooner than later. I was not prepared and had no idea what I was in for.

7

The Calm Before the Storm

They say right before a tsunami hits there is usually an earthquake and then the water level recedes from the shores. 2008 was my earthquake—a precursor filled with storms warning me of the tsunami that was headed my way.

It started with a call from the IRS asking me to come to the office. I found myself sitting in an empty, windowless, cold room at a small table for two people— kind of like the rooms you see on *The First 48* television show where homicide detectives interrogate their suspects.

The energy was off, and I had no idea what any of this was about. Even though I knew I didn't owe any taxes, my intuition warned me this wasn't right.

A middle-aged gentleman walked into the room and proceeded to ask me several questions to confirm my identity including the address of my club. Afterward, he stepped out of the office, and the few minutes I was alone waiting for him to come back was enough to get my heart racing. I felt myself getting fidgety from the anticipation. I was certain at this point something was wrong.

He came back in the room scowling at me and slid a $100,000 tax collection bill in front of me and asked when they could be paid. My first thought was something had to be wrong. My partners assured me we were up to date on all our bills. As I stared at the collection notice, I could feel my throat tightening up and the room didn't feel so cold anymore. For the first time in years, I was really worried.

I asked him if I could have some time to discuss the situation with my business partners. After he agreed, I couldn't get out of there fast enough.

As I walked back to my office, I started thinking about what just happened and the decrease in sales that we'd been noticing in the last six months at the club. I started wondering if maybe this IRS thing had some truth to it, and maybe I wasn't being told everything. I knew I didn't double-check the numbers. I trusted what my business partners told me every Monday during our weekly meetings. I hadn't even questioned it until now. I decided to wait to discuss this with any of them until after I have an audit done on the books. I wanted the straight facts before I approached anyone and just got their excuses.

Within a day or two, I got another surprise call. This time it was the State Tax Board of Equalization wanting to schedule a meeting with me about my $230,000 tax bill that was due. I damn near fell off the fucking chair. This time though, instead of my throat closing, I could feel the anger rising. That call was validation that something wasn't right, and I was positive I had been lied to. One thing I can't stomach is the coward act of secrecy and hiding when I've given someone my trust, and that's exactly what this felt like.

I scheduled that appointment to meet immediately, and it went the same as the previous one at the IRS. This time, though, I walked out feeling as if life was surreal and I was drowning in a problem much bigger than I knew how to handle.

I immediately went for a drink. One drink led to two drinks, and that led to a whole night of binge drinking. It was my temporary attempt to drown my problems in hopes that they'd disappear when I woke up in the morning.

Of course, the opposite happened. I could hear my phone continuously buzzing. It was well before 10 a.m., and anyone in the nightlife industry knows you don't call a club owner before 10 a.m. Anyone who doesn't know that wasn't worth answering for in my world. So I ignored it, but the damn thing wouldn't stop buzzing. My head was pounding and spinning, and I forced myself to climb out of bed to turn the damn thing off. Then I saw who it was. It was Walt, the man I leased the building from for the Vault.

I knew that it must be an emergency if he was calling me at this hour, and the first thought that came to my mind was that the building was on fire. "Hey Walt, what's going on?" I had to muster every ounce of energy that I could just to sound halfway normal. "I don't know you tell me. I haven't been paid rent in the past six months. I've just been getting partial payments and I need to know what's going on."

I paused for a minute in disbelief that quickly turned to nausea. I almost fell off the bed, and I could feel the stress regurgitating in my throat as I tried to collect myself.

"I did not know that, Walt. I'm going to come to your office right now and we're going to fix this," I assured him.

I hung up the phone thinking *what the holy fuck is going on?* I felt like I was stuck in some kind of nightmare I couldn't wake up from.

Walt was not only pissed but disappointed in me. I knew he believed me when I shook his hand and told him I wouldn't let him down. Now here I was trying to explain to him why I'd let him down, and even more embarrassing, how I wasn't even aware of the situation. I owed him $80,000 in rent, and I left Walt's office with a heavy cloud of shame hanging over me. I hated the fact that out of anyone, this man who took my word on a handshake, was caught in the middle of this storm.

I immediately called Harry, my mentor. He advised me to have the bookkeeper do a full audit for the past year. I still hadn't told any of my partners because I didn't want to alert anyone that I knew what was going on. I started gathering my facts the next day when the bookkeeper came into the office. I went straight to her and demanded to know what was going on.

She had been my bookkeeper from the previous endeavors that I'd had with other clubs, and I was under the assumption that her loyalty was to me. Apparently, that assumption was wrong because she

explained to me she didn't feel it was her place to disclose the standing of the business directly to me, and that she had advised my partners of the severity of the situation. She ran the report and I called Doug, Winston, Regina, and Harry arranging an emergency meeting Monday morning.

That weekend I reviewed the audit report and learned one of my partners was funding another business with the money from the Vault, and even though it wasn't extreme amounts, it was significant enough to have an effect. The careless behavior was written all over the report. As the owner, I had to take responsibility for my careless behavior. I should have been checking the books. I should have been checking everything.

I went into the meeting Monday morning wearing what I call my uniform—jeans and a white V-neck t-shirt, holding a big black binder with the report. Everyone was sitting at the conference table with guilt written all over their faces. I had time over the weekend to accept the situation and started the meeting off saying, "I think we all got off track. We don't love ourselves and our company like we did when we started with the attitude to dominate the nightlife business and change San Jose."

They all looked at me confused, and I spelled out what had surfaced last week. Everyone's heads were hanging down, validating that they knew and no one had much to say. I knew then that the party had taken over, the money got to all of our heads, and this meeting was a slap in our faces to wake up.

8

The
Tsunami

August 8, 2008, (8-8-8), the bank levied our corporate accounts with $40,000, just enough to pay our employees' salaries. I immediately went into action mode and went to a bankruptcy attorney named Charles Logan, who was referred to me by a friend. He advised me to file a skeleton Chapter 11 bankruptcy so our funds were given back while we reorganized the company. But his retainer was $20,000, which I didn't have. In a flurry, I left and borrowed from anyone and everyone I could. I came back to his office with a paper bag filled with $20,000. I left with a receipt and some assurance that it would be handled.

30 days later, I turned on the news to find that my prestigious, well-known Silicon Valley

Bankruptcy attorney committed suicide. He was found shot in the head and the car was set on fire, and no one knew why. They ruled it a suicide. Right when I thought my world couldn't crash down any harder, it did.

My case was taken over by another attorney, Charles Green, who wanted another $20,000 retainer to continue with my case. I left his office again like a mad man on a hunt, borrowed my life away on the coattails of my good name, and came back to his office with another $20,000 payment.

I stopped paying my mortgage. I let my Ferrari and cars get repossessed. I was driving a white cargo van with no idea or plan on how I was going to change this situation. Every day seemed like a living nightmare with absolutely no light at the end of the tunnel. During those times, I realized who my friends really were.

My phone used to constantly ring with people who acted as if they cared, but now that I had lost everything, the silence of my phone was another reminder that my life had quickly flipped on me like a bad joke.

Still, no matter what, I never let anyone see me sweat. Maintaining my composure at all times has always been a rule for me. Anything other than that I consider weakness.

I knew there were people, and still are, who would take great pleasure in seeing me down and out. Therefore, I've never let that happen, and I always give the perception I have my shit under control. One thing I know about myself is when I have my back up against the wall, I'll fight and do everything in my power to make things right. In 2008

I was relying purely on this fact that I knew about myself.

It seemed like the whole world was in a panic with the recession in full effect, so many getting evicted, and the buzz and swirl of President Obama's election taking place. It felt as if there was no corner to turn to for peace. The heavy energy of depression, frustration, and misery were so thick everywhere.

April 4, 2009, there I was sitting on the floor in my shower, butt naked, sobbing like a child with no answers, and no idea what the fuck I was going to do. All I knew is that I was giving up the keys to my house today. I knew that the bank was giving me a check for $5,000 in exchange for me vacating the premises. I knew that I was getting in my white cargo van with $5,000 in my pocket and reluctantly going couch surfing in the living rooms of the few friends I was grateful to have left.

My old friend, Sal Flores, a mentor and former partner of a popular San Jose Latin nightclub, called Miami's and graciously invited me to stay with him in his 7,500 square foot mansion in the Almaden Valley.

He had a thriving construction development business and started utilizing my assistance immediately. I thought I had dodged a bullet in life, and that my comeback was going to be linked to Sal in some way. I found myself being his personal assistant and driver. He would be on his phone conducting business, and I noticed that there was always a lot of chaos around him because of the way he did business.

That should have been a red flag to me, but I was still stuck in my old ways of not caring enough to stop and pay attention, completely functioning out of my ego as if nothing else could happen to me. I continued functioning with the cocky attitude that I could slide out of any situation because I thought

I could. Therefore, my reaction was to turn a blind eye, let it pass, and keep going. It was all about to implode rather than learning the lesson that the situation was trying to teach me. All I was focused on was for an opportunity to present itself, and it did.

During one of Sal's meetings, I started talking to a guy connected with Westfield Shopping Center, and I pitched the idea of having an eclectic bar lounge called REPUBLIKA at Valley Fair Mall across the street from Santana Row. We were going into the biggest recession in U.S. history; 2008-2009 turned the world of finance upside down.

Every business was trying to figure out ways to drive more traffic to their location since people were not out spending money the same way they used to. I knew that. I also knew that with Santana Row being the newest hit place in San Jose and located right across the street from the mall, it was a perfect opportunity to leverage the traffic from there to the mall area through creating a nightlife spot in the shopping center.

The guy pitched it to Westfield Shopping Center, and they were sold on the idea. They even offered to give me four more Westfield mall locations to build this concept at Downtown San Francisco, Valencia, La Jolla, and Topanga. This was the exact break I needed. They agreed to reimburse a certain amount of money after it was built, so I needed to find funding and build my team. I immediately started contacting people in the industry that I knew would love to work with me on this project, and Sal and I agreed to be 50/50 partners on it.

I not only got all the funding we needed up to $100 million, but I built the entire team of people I knew who trusted me and were experts in their field. I brought in a strong attorney and accountant to represent us and a strong financial arm to give us the funding we needed.

Everything was in place, and once again, I felt like I had dodged a major bullet in life. I was in the "go, go, go" mindset, reacting out of desperation, and just wanting to scrape my way out of the small blip in my life instead of taking time to think it all through.

All that momentum soon came to a halt with three calls that seemed eerily similar to the three calls I received earlier in the year from the IRS and State Board of Equalization and Walt. The attorney who I brought in on the project called and asked me how my relationship was with Sal. When I asked him why, he told me he didn't see my name on the paperwork as a true partner, minority shareholder.

Shortly afterward, I received a call from the accountant I brought in on the team who let me know he was putting the paperwork together for the corporation structure and saw that I'm more of a junior partner.

I was still thinking of how to confront Sal on this when I received a third call from one of the funders I brought in who asked if I was aware that Sal was holding meetings and making some big decisions with the team without me, and trying to tell everyone I authorized it because I knew he would take care of me. He let me know every single person participating in this project was willing to fund this thing, but that they weren't going to do it if it wasn't for me.

It was like déjà vu, and I started recognizing a pattern that was reoccurring in my life. I realized I needed to slow down and be more methodical in business. There's a process of getting things done the right way. When you rush, you get rushed results, which leads to things crashing. I needed to get answers before moving forward; otherwise, I'd be setting myself up for another, perhaps bigger fall. If I was going to bring resources, if I was going to get this thing funded, I wanted to make sure that I'm a 50/50 partner. Something that I've learned from one of my mentors is that if we walk, we all walk together. It has to be fair.

I wrote Sal a letter telling him I notified the entire team that everything is on hold, including the funds, until I tell them otherwise. I gave him a list of questions I needed an answer to before moving forward with the project. Questions that included: What was my role in the project? What were everyone's roles in the project? What were the expectations he had of everyone? I told him I'd be returning after the weekend in order for us to discuss all of this.

I knew he ran early in the morning, so I left the letter by his running shoes and left for the weekend to LA. When I returned, instead of answers from him, I received only extreme hostility because he was being confronted and the funds were on hold.

He was clearly aggravated and defensive and acted as if he felt entitled to being sole partner, which I later discovered that he was planning on using the funds for that project to fund another business. Again, eerily similar to what happened to me with the Vault. It turned into a semi-physical altercation. Within minutes, our friendship, partnership, and project were completely ruined.

I packed my things up from his house and got into my Ford Focus to go back to LA to my sister's house with only $40 in my pocket. I had finally hit rock bottom.

9

The Smoke & Mirrors

went to my sister's house ashamed and embarrassed. All my life she had seen me win and gain massive success. She knew this was my rock bottom and opened her home to me with zero judgment. She gave me her spare room in the house. It was small, but it was mine for now. The bed was just a full size mattress with just a box spring on the floor. There was a small desk, chair, and dresser, and that's it.

I immediately hung up the whiteboard I brought with me. I'm a visual person and I knew I was going to draw and write myself out of this problem.

That first night, I laid there completely stripped of everything I've ever worked for and thought I was no longer Mr. Successful that could bounce back from my biggest loss. I had lost. I felt lost and it all hit me, but I realize now that it was exactly what I needed. I needed to get humble, and I did.

I knew I had no money, so I applied for unemployment. I knew I needed to be around people that had the entrepreneurial spirit, who I could learn from so I could climb my way out. I immediately contacted people I knew in the nightlife industry in LA. None of them could believe I was asking for a job in their bar or nightclub. They all said I was overqualified, they couldn't pay me what I'm worth, and they were in shock I was even asking because they knew all the success I had gained in the Bay Area. I told them I'd take anything because, at that point, I just wanted to stay busy, get out of my head, and find a way to get back in the game. People can sense when you're acting out of desperation, fear, and I think they sensed it. No one offered me an opportunity.

I did have this one friend, Rick Martin, who owned a successful streetwear company, and I thought it was interesting. I asked him to let me work with him and learn, and he could just pay me for my gas there and back home. He agreed.

I stopped drinking. I stopped going out at night. Everything stopped. I was completely dialed into my routine. I'd get up at 5:30 a.m., go to 24 Hour Fitness, and work out. I'd get ready at the gym and then drive to Rick's warehouse in Downtown LA where I worked all day basically doing inventory, folding clothes, and loading boxes.

My car became a mobile university. I stopped listening to music, and all I listened to was motivational and self-development videos. I was the hungriest I'd ever been and was determined to get my mind right so I could manifest my way out of this dark hole.

I would sit in my room writing on my whiteboard what I wanted my life to look like, ideas, inspirational quotes, and anything that kept my spirits up. I'd lay on the bed and stare at this whiteboard visioning what I want. I knew me believing that I could get out of this situation was half of the battle. I refused to believe that my life was ruined and that the current circumstance I was in was going to consume me. I knew I was going to get out of it. I didn't see how. Everything around me said it was dire, but I chose to believe that it wasn't. I chose to believe that this circumstance is a temporary stopping point to teach me a lesson, so I must find what the lesson is and learn it. I knew it was that belief that is the recipe to succeed.

I still had Detox Sundays at the DoubleTree Hotel, so every month I had to drive up to San Jose to host the party. No one knew I moved to LA. Everyone still thought I was this big-shot party promoter, and for me, this was a good thing.

I needed to keep my reputation. I let everyone think that. I kept my cool and never disclosed what I was really going through. It was difficult, and most of the time I felt completely alone.

Everyone saw me dressed nicely in freshly shined shoes, but no one knew the bottom of my shoes had holes. No one knew I was calculating my miles and gas to be sure I could make it back home to LA. No one knew I was living off unemployment and the little money I made on Detox Sundays toward the end of that era. No one knew that I was fighting for my life.

LA is a different beast. In San Jose, I'm a big shark in a small ocean, but in LA, you're a big shark with other big sharks that are bigger than you in a bigger ocean. Really, I was a fish in a shark tank. It's a different world. In LA, if you don't grow up there or find a niche or a certain area that you're in- you're lost. I was trying to reach my roots, but my roots had been so uprooted from LA. I realized my roots were really in San Jose and the Bay Area, and that if I was going to find another opportunity, it was going to be there.

In 2011, I got into my car I called my "mobile university" and made my way back home to San Jose. I called a friend of mine who had an inflatable mattress and living room he said I could stay in, and I took it. I knew with a new mindset, a new opportunity would present itself sooner than later. I just needed to be ready and available.

10

New Beginnings

Your mind is a muscle, and it will think how you train it to think. I was on a mission to build my brain muscle whatever way I could. I continued to religiously listen to all kinds of self-development videos after I came back to San Jose. I felt like I was getting myself ready for battle so I'd be ready when my next chance came, and it did.

I had become extremely humbled by my situation, and if I had forgotten to be, the holes on the bottom of my shoes reminded me.

I was measuring my days and weeks by how much gas I had in my tank. I knew how much my car needed to fill up. I calculated every decision and location that I had to go to. Every move I made was strategic.

I had moved in with my long-time friend Jorge Sanchez, owner of Chachos restaurant in Campbell. He was having a falling out with his business partner, and I suggested he relocate his restaurant back to Downtown San Jose where it all started.

I found the perfect location and once again we needed to raise the funds. One of my buddies knew a guy who would be interested and gave me his contact information. His name was Terrence Brown. He was a tall guy, African American, very well educated, and very smooth. It was the fastest deal I had ever closed.

Jorge and I went to meet him at his office in one of the tall buildings in the PruneYard in Campbell. As I was introducing Jorge and myself and telling him about our professional background, he cut me off and said he knew who we were and asked how much we needed. I was completely taken aback and gave him the first number that came to my head. I told him we needed $150,000 to start. He asked if we needed it all now or if he could split it up and give us half today and a half in a few days.

I said, "Yeah you can give us half now and we will take the other half in a couple of days." He reached into his cabinet, pulled out a blank check, started writing, and asked who he should make it out to. I had to stop him for a second because it seemed unreal that we were collecting a check for $75,000 this easy. I mean, we'd only been in his office less than 20 minutes. "Wait a minute," I said. "Do you want us to set up an LLC or some kind of agreement?" He said, "No, I know where to find you." He was smooth.

I whispered to Jorge right when we got in the elevator not to celebrate, not to make any moves, cause he was probably watching us through the windows. We didn't crack a smile or look like we just got our asses saved. We kept our cool, but as soon as we got in the car, we were like two little kids in a toy store.

January 19, 2012, Chacho's at the Downtown San Jose location opened. It was the start of a new beginning for me when we cut the ribbon on opening day. I was back.

Soon afterward, I got my own flat in Downtown San Jose. It was beautiful. I fixed it up to have a similar style and colors that my previous flat had—red walls, chocolate brown hallways. It was my place.

A few years later, I met my soon to be business partner, Lance. We started California Labor Force on January 1, 2014, a staffing company that serves the construction, demolition, asbestos abatement, and disaster removal industries. I had no clue what I was about to embark onto.

I never thought I'd be the founder of a company that would soon have six offices spread throughout California with over 1,000 employees when I was laying on the small bed at my sister's house a few years earlier.

The same year we opened California Labor Force, I co founded LATINLIFE.com. An online media company targeting the Latino consumer. Life changed for me and it allowed to get my condo in the high-rise building in Downtown San Jose, surrounded by windows that overlooked the city along with the Silicon Valley. I remember walking into my new home completely filled with gratitude.

I realized my money was a by-product of my hard work. I learned I have life-long tools that no one will ever be able to strip me of. They can take my money or business, but they can't take away what I know. I know that consistency is always the key. You have to stay consistent in your tasks and your goals, staying focused on what you want in life.

If you're not consistent, you're not going to get anywhere. You have to keep that pressure on all the time so you can keep yourself dialed in and not deviate from the goals and outcomes.

I live life like I have ten targets and ten bullets like a sniper. I can't afford to miss a target because once I miss that target, I become a target. I'll do whatever it takes to not miss the target, and part of that is slowing down and being patient. I've always been patient, but through the years I've really learned to master the art of patience.

I'm that guy who will sit at the chair and wait for you all day just to have that conversation. I can outpatient anyone. While I'm waiting, my vision is becoming strong, so strong, in fact, that when I finally get the conversation—it's a wrap.

The energy from my visions have become so strong I realize it's been magnetic for people around me. It's power. My good friend and mentor, Marshall Jones, says that if I told everyone that if they jumped off a building they'd fly, people would jump off. I don't know if it's necessarily true to that extent, but there's definitely a strong pulsating energy from my beliefs.

Anything I say, I believe. I'm either all in or all out. I don't talk about it unless I believe it. If I believe it, then I know it's already done.

Everything I've been through was preparing me for this. I've always been a leader. Even growing up, I had to lead my own way. I've always believed I'm only as good as my team, and for us to rise, we all have to rise up together. Stedman Graham said to me once while we shared some words, "In order to lead others, you must learn to lead yourself first."

I never think I'm better than anyone else. One of the clichés I believe, even though it's cheesy, is that there is no "I" in "Team."

In order to really be all in with your team, you must trust them, and sometimes this can be a dou-ble-edged sword because, at the end of the day, money makes people act weird. You start noticing people acting differently around you, and then you start questioning what and who is real.

You can't live your life with your guard up either because then you'll never have a true team. So, there's always a risk when you let people into your energy field. I learned that trusting myself comes first. Believing I now know how to honor my instinctual feelings, know when to slow down, when to take a step back and reanalyze, and most importantly, when to let go.

I'm not going to pretend I know for sure what is next, or where I'll be in five or ten years. One thing I do know for certain is that I finally reintroduced that young, ambitious boy from LA who was hungry to be myself again, and he's not ever going away.

TO BE CONTINUED.........

Mauricio Mejia

Entrepreneur – Speaker –
Mentor – Philanthropist

What does he stand for? Excellence—and an inde-
fatigable energy to do what is best and what's next.
Mauricio utilizes his day, every day, to maximize
the momentum of his enterprise and to give back
to those who desire to learn from his upsides and
his downturns. How? He studies and learns, he
decides, and he commits and executes. He expects

nothing less from those with whom he surrounds himself.

Known originally as the "Godfather of San Jose Nightlife," he earned his first million by age 25. He's now known as a man who learned and continues to grow into one of the foremost visionaries of Silicon Valley. From gang life and homelessness to a mogul creating an empire, he realized the compassion and the empathy to do more for his community and his culture to create an economic standard that propels leadership and success. In the same room with him, you will always rise to your very best. With kindness, he advises. With love, he shows vulnerability. With the discernment and creativity of a survivor, he thrives…and he will ensure the same for you.